Falling Daisies

Ebony Davis

BookLeaf Publishing

Presentation by *BookLeaf Publishing*

Web: www.bookleafpub.com

E-mail: info@bookleafpub.com

ISBN: 9789357447195

First edition 2021

DEDICATION

Dedicated to those who believed in me and to those who doubted me,

I am everything and more, because of you.

ACKNOWLEDGEMENT

I would like to acknowledge those who believed in me most, My darling mother (Letitia), My loving Grandma (Margaret) and the light in my life, My Grandpa (Neil). Without them, I would not exist, nor would I have the courage to face each day. They all believed in me when most did not, They encouraged me to continue when I faltered, They told me I was worth it; and to me, that meant everything.

To my dear friend Brody, I thank you for all that you are and all that you mean to me.

To the friends of my soul, Riv, Em, Jo, Weezy, Eris, Paula, Laura, Joey and all the rest of you beautiful people, Thank you for always being there. Thank you for showing me the light in life, for reminding me how to laugh and how to have fun. Thank you for encouraging me in all that I do and validating me when I feel doubt. You are all so very special and I am forever grateful to know you.

Especially dedicated to the most wonderful man i have ever known, without you i am not sure how i will go on; but i will. For you. Grandpa, you will always be in my heart and I will carry you with me for always.

PREFACE

This collection of poetry was written immediately following a monumental loss in my life. Though I have struggled with sadness and all the different facets of such emotion throughout my life, this wave of grief hit me differently.

With this collection of poetry, good or bad, I hope to be able to show you, the reader, a small insight into the confusing, often dark and sad place, that is my mind.

This will be a true reflection of me and my hope is that, by the end of this, you feel as if you understand.

If there is one thing I feel you should know before reading on, it is this.

Fear not the unpaved, the rough, the uncertain.
Fear not the dark, the shadows, the night.
Instead, embrace all that dwells within it, for it will show you the path to the light.

Empty

I had thought,
I'd felt empty before.
Now I know that is not true.

Because the loss of you,
It all feels new.
And I really wish it didn't.

Suddenly

It is quite strange,
How quickly life can change.
When you stop to think,
Or when you take time to blink.
One moment you were here,
The next and you weren't.

I saw you, just yesterday.
You were here, you were present.
I knew that this would happen one day,
That you would be gone.
Just that, despite knowing it,
I had hoped, i would never have to,
Live it.

No Goodbye, Shared Farewell

I did not get to say goodbye,
I did not get the chance.
You were gone before i even blinked,
Before I got a second glance.

When next i saw you, laying there.
Pale, Quiet and Still.
It seemed to me, You'd shrunken,
From a mountain, to a hill.

Your skin, it felt quite waxy.
Ice cold and stretched too taut.
Such a strange sharp contrast,
To the warmth you always brought.

Family gathered throughout the room,
On video call as well.
The love for you that binds us,
As we gathered to say farewell.

Missed

My heart broke, when we lost you,
Though you did not leave alone.
For most of me went with you.
Time of death, Time of peace,
Unknown.

Forever we will miss you,
Most days we will cry.
For if love alone could have saved you,
You never would have died.

We travelled to the service,
Arrangements made with care.
We all shared such heartache,
When we turned and left you there.

If our tears could create a window,
Our heartache, create a door.
We would walk on through,
Just to be with you,
To hug you,
Just once more.

Think of you again

When i feel the sun,
and it warms my skin,
I think of you again.

When i hear a tune,
And i sing along,
I think of you again.

Each time i see a flock of birds,
Or see a dog walk by,
Or when the wind,
Starts whispering,
I think of you again.

Times of Quiet

It is the moments when the world is asleep,
and the day is finally done.
When the day no longer keeps me busy,
And everyone is at rest,
That I can think of you.

When all the noise has faded,
And all the voices go quiet,
That i sit and let,
My mind fall open,
And I fill it up with you.

Taught

My Father you were not,
Though our bond was special still.
Losing you, Tears me in two,
Your dreams, I will fulfill.

I will be strong and funny and kind,
Just like you taught me to be.
I'll sing a song and dance along,
Like no one is watching me.

Through the years

Through the years,
You've always been,
A brilliant man to me.

From when i was small,
And you helped me stand tall.
To when i was older and needed a shoulder,
You never let me fall.

You helped me get through,
And i am just lucky to have known,
As special a Grandpa as you.

Understood

You always understood me,
Always knew just what to say.
You always made me smile,
When my world was coloured grey.

You took me to the markets,
The festivals and shows.
You even taught me how to drive,
Even if you dozed.

We had so many adventures,
Got up to mischief too.
If i had to describe it,
I was the feathers and you,
You were the glue.

Stars

I saw a clear night sky,
Where the stars shone so bright,
And I thought of you.

See, the stars bring me peace,
Bring my mind to a stop.
The flickering,
The flaring,
Like connecting the dots.

I picture a thousand and one things,
In the sky.
Most of them memories,
I let the sadness float by.

I lay on the ground,
I stare up at the stars,
I think you would enjoy this.

Wherever you are,
I hope you see them too,
And that you are finally at peace.

Voices

Sometimes i hear these whispers,
Echo in my ear.
Sometimes it's as loud as shouting,
Sounding quite so very near.
Sometimes it is from far away,
and I strain to hear it.
The strangest thing, i'd have to say,
I think Pa's the one who does it.

Dear

From the time the sun rises,
Till the time it sets.
From when i open my eyes,
And when I close them to rest.
It is thoughts of you,
That wander through,
All my thoughts and dreams.
I hold you close,
Within my heart,
For you are very dear.
Though now you're gone,
I will carry on,
To my soul, you are near.

When i was younger

When i was younger,
You took me to the snow.
Let me slide down the hill,
Oh so very slow.

Then you got this gleam in your eyes,
As you showed me a bag,
On which i could sled,
And you watched as i sped,
Fast down the hill,
Right into the snowman's head.

Your Anniversary

A day in October,
Nineteen-sixty-eight,
Was the day that you married Grandma.

Your anniversary has arrived,
And it breaks my heart,
From seeing her cry.

No Time

Sometimes i feel,
Like I have no time to mourn.
Having to be strong,
The one they lean on.

Their loss feels so much more worse than mine,
So why should I not give up my time?

Time goes by

Minutes turn into hours,
Hours into days,
Days into weeks.

Weeks turn into months,
And months turn into years.
In time the pain will lesson,
Though never truly clear.

New Normal

I hate the new normal.
The one where you're not here.
I want to walk right backwards,
To when you would be here.

I know it is supposed to,
Get easier every day.
But i don't want to let go,
I'll miss you either way.

Pa's Garden

Our Pa created a garden,
A garden from his heart.
He tended and planted,
Gave our lives,
And their start.

He covered us in sunshine,
Gave life to hopes and dreams.
He nurtured every little seed,
And grew our self-esteem.

When time saw the wind,
The storms and the rain.
He covered us in shelter,
protected just enough,
Gave us what we needed,
To grow brave and strong and tough.

He was our good example,
Though he had his mischief too.
He taught us what we needed,
What is right, from what is wrong.
Lessons for us to carry,
All of our lives long.

We are our Grandpa's Garden,
Tended lovingly and with care.
We are our Grandpa's legacy.
And his memory we will share.

www.ingramcontent.com/pod-product-compliance
Lightning Source LLC
Chambersburg PA
CBHW062111140826
49812CB00058B/1264
* 9 7 8 9 3 5 7 4 4 7 1 9 5 *